WITHDRAWN

Russell Stannard

The Lab Cats See the Light

A look at light and sound

Illustrated by
Bill Ledger

MARSHALL PUBLISHING • LONDON

Note to Parents

This **Lab Cats** book introduces the ideas of light and sound to young children in an enjoyable way as they follow the adventures of a gang of cats. It can be read aloud while a younger child follows the words and pictures, or an older child can read it alone. Each experiment that the cats do is followed by the correct answers. Ask your child to give the answer before turning the page to see what the Lab Cats did. Any new or difficult scientific words are explained in "What the Words Mean" on page 36. Happy reading!

A Marshall Edition
Conceived, edited and designed by
Marshall Editions Ltd
The Orangery
161 New Bond Street
London W1S 2UF
www.marshallpublishing.com

First published in the UK in 2001 by
Marshall Publishing Ltd

10 9 8 7 6 5 4 3 2 1

ISBN 1 84028 551 6

Originated in the UK by Hilo
Printed in Portugal by Printer Portuguesa

Editor: Rosalind Beckman
Managing Designer: Caroline Sangster
Art Director: Simon Webb
Editorial Manager: Janet Sacks
US Consultant: Dr Roberta Butler
Production: Christina Schuster

It was the middle of the night. All was dark – except for the school science laboratory. Prof, the caretaker's cat, was taking a lesson.

Earlier that day, she had listened carefully to what the teacher had been telling the children. Now it was her turn to pass on what she had learned to her own class. It was her way of keeping young cats off the street at night.

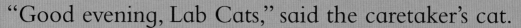

"Good evening, Lab Cats," said the caretaker's cat.

"Good evening, Prof," they replied.

"Are we all here?" she asked.

One by one they called out their names.

"What are we going to do tonight?" asked Swot.

"Today the children learned about light. Let's begin by thinking about where light comes from. Any ideas?"

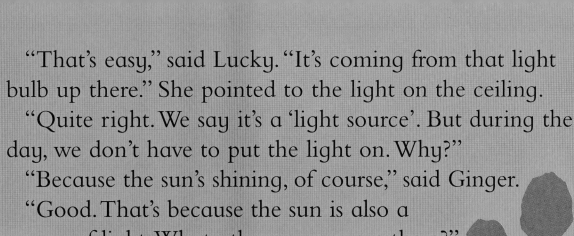

"That's easy," said Lucky. "It's coming from that light bulb up there." She pointed to the light on the ceiling.

"Quite right. We say it's a 'light source'. But during the day, we don't have to put the light on. Why?"

"Because the sun's shining, of course," said Ginger.

"Good. That's because the sun is also a source of light. What other sources are there?"

Can you think of any other examples of light sources?

Precious!

Ginger!

Lucky!

Basher!

"Excellent!" declared the Prof. "Those all give out light. We see the light when it enters our eyes."

"I can see you…and the others…and the room," said Ginger. "Does that mean we are all light sources?"

"No," replied the Prof. "We are not giving out any light of our own. You see us and the other things only by the light coming from the bulb up there. The light is reflecting – or bouncing – off us. If the light is switched off, you no longer see us. We will be in darkness."

11

"What about darkness?" asked Ginger. "Where does it come from?"

"Darkness is simply what you get when there is no light," explained the Prof. "Now let's have a look at the way light travels away from a source. We'll use this torch."

The Prof laid the torch down on the bench top. She then held a comb in front of it.

"There!" she exclaimed. "Watch what happens to the rays of light when they pass through the gaps between the teeth of this comb."

The Prof drew a picture on the board. "Why can't the mother see the boy?" she asked.

"Because he's hiding round the corner," replied Ginger.

"Yes. The light reflecting from the boy travels in straight lines. Light cannot bend round corners," the Prof explained.

"It could with a mirror," suggested Swot.

"Good point," said the Prof. "Let's see how mirrors work. Who is going to help me?"

Swot and Lucky placed a mirror in the path of a ray of light. The ray of light changed direction.

"You see that?" the Prof asked. "Now, can anyone tell me why you can see your face when you look in a mirror?"

Look! It's changing direction!

"The light leaving your face is reflected back to you by the mirror," said Basher.

"Cars and buses have mirrors," said Fluff.

"That's right," agreed the Prof. "They are placed at different angles so the driver can see what is happening behind and to the side.

"Now look at what happens to words when they are reflected in a mirror."

"They are written backwards!" exclaimed Lucky.

"That's because reflections switch left and right," the Prof explained. "I have written some words backwards on these cards. Look at them in a mirror to see what they say."

Can you guess what the words on the board say?

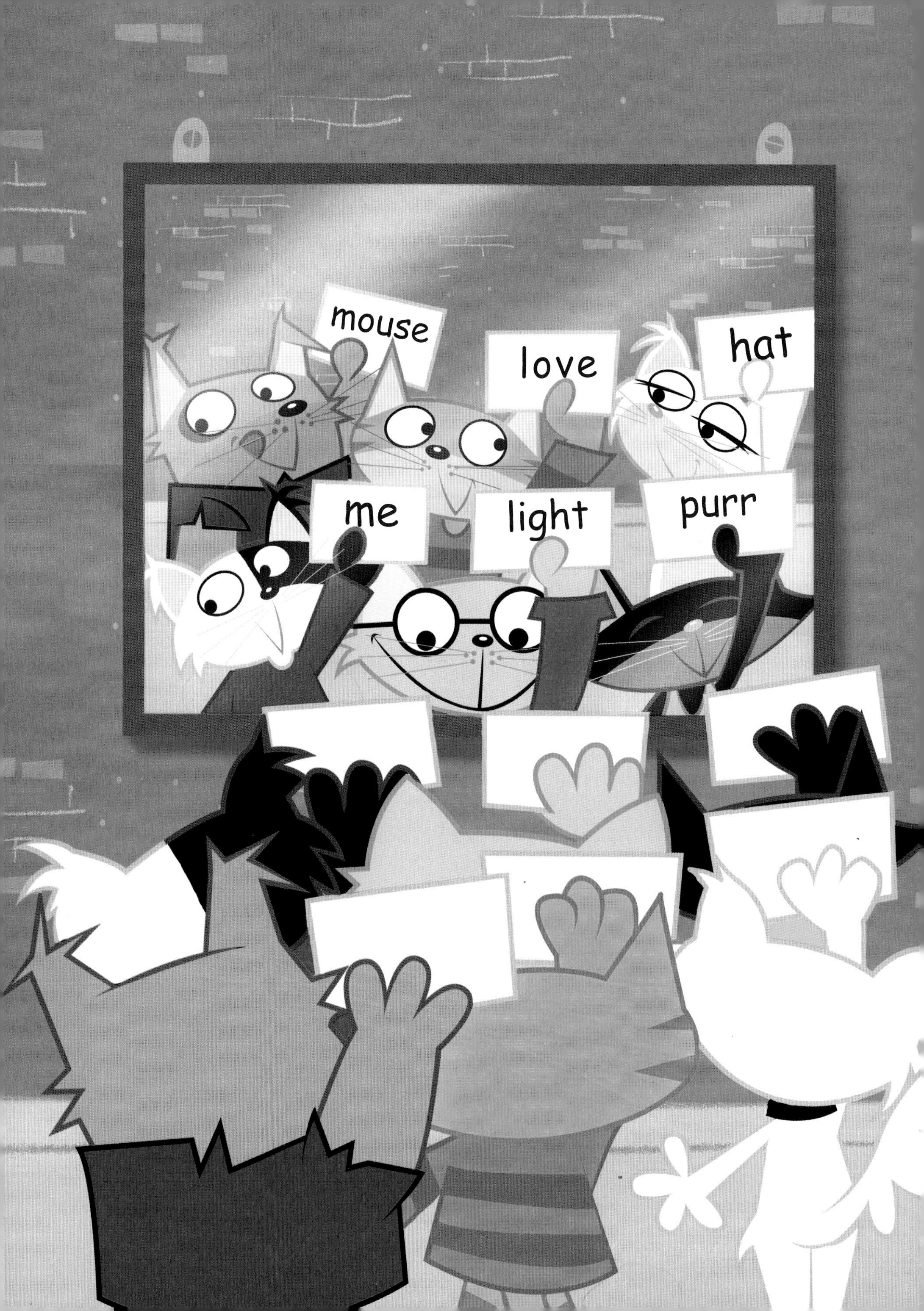
mouse
love
hat
me
light
purr

"You can see reflections in lots of shiny surfaces," continued the Prof. "If the surfaces are curved, not flat, you can look funny."

"Light can pass through some things, but not through others," said the Prof. "Light can pass through glass, for example. We can see through it. We call these things *transparent*. When light cannot pass through things, we call them *opaque*. Opaque things cast shadows."

"I know how to make shadows," said Basher, with a wicked grin.

He held up his paws, and there on the wall was a shadow picture of – a DOG!

"That's quite enough of that, Basher!" said the Prof crossly. "Now here are some pictures. I want you to decide which of these things are transparent and which opaque."

"The children also learned about sound today," the Prof said. "Here are some sound sources. They are instruments for making music. Who knows how to play a tune?"

None of the Lab Cats had ever played a musical instrument before – but that did not stop them from trying. What a noise they made!

Musical instruments make sounds. Can you think of other sources of sound?

"With some instruments, like drums, triangles and cymbals, you have to hit them to make a sound," said the Prof. "We call them percussion instruments."

"Purr...cussion?" murmured Lucky, purring happily.

"Some instruments, like violins and guitars, have strings that move, or vibrate," she told them.

She showed the Lab Cats how to make a one-stringed guitar using a thick fishing line. Precious plucked the string and it gave out a note.

She experimented by pulling the string tighter. The note was higher. She then moved the pencil nearer the table edge and tried again.

"You can make other kinds of instruments, too," said the Prof. "Pour some water into these glasses and tap them gently. The sound of the note will depend on the amount of water in the glass."

Lucky poured some water into a wine glass and ran a wet paw round its rim. It gave out a beautiful long note.

Swot blew across the top of a bottle.

"Your instrument makes the air next to it vibrate," said the Prof. "The vibrations then spread out through the air as sound waves. These sound waves make your eardrums vibrate. That's when you hear the sound." She set an alarm clock ringing, and placed it under a glass dome. "As I pump out the air under the dome, listen to the sound of the clock."

What do you think will happen to the sound?

The sound faded away. "There!" said the Prof. "With no air in the dome, the sound can no longer reach us."

"I know another way of making the clock sound faint." said Fluff. "You could put it further away."

"Quite right," agreed the Prof. "Sound spreads out, so when it comes from far away, your ear catches less of it.

"You can stop the sound from spreading out by speaking through a hosepipe and funnel. Or you can catch more of the sound if you listen through a funnel."

"Sound passes through other things besides air, such as water," the Prof continued. "It can also pass through thin walls, but not so easily through thick walls. Some things, such as wearing ear muffs, stop sound getting through."

Meanwhile, the Prof altered the drawing on the board. "Oh!" exclaimed Lucky. "The mother's found the boy!" "But she hasn't seen him yet," the Prof pointed out. "No, but she heard the noise," replied Ginger. "That's because sound can spread round corners. It's different from light. Light only travels in straight lines."

Just then there was a flash of lightning, followed by the distant rumble of thunder. Some of the Lab Cats looked uneasy. "Why do you always get thunder when there is lightning?" asked Basher.

"Thunder is simply the noise made when the lightning strikes," the Prof explained.

"Then why don't we hear the thunder at the same time as we see the flash?" asked Swot.

"Because sound travels more slowly than light. Sound takes longer to arrive," said the Prof. As she spoke, there was a loud CLAP of thunder – and the cats panicked.

"Let's hold a gig," suggested Basher. "That way this bunch of scaredy cats won't be able to hear the thunder."

"An excellent idea," agreed the Prof.

To tell the truth, the noise made by the Lab Cats was terrible. But no one seemed to mind. They made so much noise, they didn't notice the storm had finished.

What a performance!

Purr...formance?

"Time to go, Lab Cats!" the Prof shouted above the din.
"But we're having such fun!" they yelled back.
"You can do more science another night. But now it's time to finish. Off you go!"
"Bye, Prof. See you soon!" they called out as, one by one, they disappeared through the cat flap.

What the words mean

Light source Anything that gives out its own light, for example, the sun or a lamp.

Opaque Something is opaque if light cannot pass through it. Opaque objects cast shadows.

Percussion Percussion instruments make musical sounds when they are hit with sticks or hammers.

Reflection This is light bouncing off a surface.

Sound Sound is made when air vibrates. This makes sound waves. The sound waves spread out from the source and make your eardrums vibrate. That's when you hear the sound.

Sound source Anything that vibrates and makes a sound, for example, a drum or string.

String String instruments, like violins and guitars, make musical sounds when their strings are rubbed by a bow or plucked.

Thunder The sound made when lightning strikes. We hear thunder after we have seen the lightning flash. This is because sound travels more slowly than light – so sound takes longer to get to us.

Transparent Something is transparent if light can pass through it, and you can see clearly what is on the other side of it, for example, a pane of glass is transparent.